POLICE
TGPD

F12 FNE

SMELLING THE CORNERS
SINCE 2002

BBC Children's Books
Published by the Penguin Group
Penguin Books Ltd, 80 Strand, London, WC2R 0RL, England
Penguin Group (Australia) Ltd, 250 Camberwell Road, Camberwell,
Victoria 3124, Australia (a division of Pearson Australia Group Pty Ltd)
Canada, India, New Zealand, South Africa

Published by BBC Children's Books, 2014
Text and design © Children's Character Books, 2014

001 – 10 9 8 7 6 5 4 3 2 1

Written by Dan Newman
Designed by Perfect Bound Ltd
Illustrations p.10 Clive Goodyer

ISBN: 978–140–591836–7

Printed in Italy

Picture credits: All photos © BBC Worldwide except the following (page numbering runs left to right, top to bottom) © Shutterstock: p.6-5 Christopher Halloran;
p.7-1 Bernhard Richte; p.7-2 Bildagentur Zoonar GmbH; p.7-3 Nicram Sabod; p.7-4 Oleg Bakhirev; p.7-5 Andrei Pop; p.7-6 Jill Lang; p.9 (fridge) Silberkorn; p.9 (duck)
Aksenova Natalya; p.9 (receipt) Bronwyn Photo; p.20-1 (wig) SSSCCC; p.20-3 Africa Studio; p.20-5 ZRyzner; p.20-6 abimages; p.21-4 Darren Brode; p.34-1 Mamuka
Gotsiridze; p.34-2 spirit of america; p.34-3 Tracy Starr; p.34-4 Africa Studio; p.34-5 Bizroug; p.34-6 K-Kwan Kwanchai; p.34-7 Ahjelika Gr; p.34-8 Luis Santos; p.34-9
James Steidl; p.34-10 Gualtiero Boffi; p.34-11 Ian 2010; p.34-12 Bikeworldtravel; p.46 Filip Robert; p.48-1 Joe Gough; p.48-2 Abramova Kseniya; p.48-3 steamroller_
blues; p.48-4 tmcphotos; p.48-5 Gaspar Janos; p.48-6 antb; p.48-7 Luis Santos; p.48-8 Tutti Frutti; p.50-2 DFree; p.50-3 Featureflash; p.50-4 David Hughes; p.50-5 K.
Miri Photography; p.50-7 Elisanth; p.50-8 Jasmin Awad; p.51-1 Lyudmyla Kharlamova; p.51-2 Robyn Mackenzie; p.51-3 & 4 Eric Isselee; p.51-5 Valentyn Volkov; p.51-6
jps; p.51-7 s_bukley; p.51-8 Featureflash; p.51-9 Ersler Dmitry; p.51-10 Dmitry Naumov; p.51-11 Eldad Carin; p.51-12 Maxx-Studio; p.51-13 Grzegorz Placzek; p.51-14
Levent Konuk; Lamborghini.com: p.41-6 & p.44-5.

CONTENTS

Introduction 2

Jeremy Reviews... 4

The Best Places to Go
For a Drive... IN THE WORLD 6

Bye-bye Beeb! 8

Stig's Fridge 9

An A-Z of *Top Gear* 10

Bus vs Supercar 12

Crossover Caravan Game 14

Richard Reviews... 16

How to Hold an All-Star Celebrity
Summer Barbecue Festival Event 18

Top Gear Judge Things 20

How to Build a HoverVan 22

The Burmese Lorrying Test 24

Italian Beauty 28

Match the Outburst 29

James Reviews... 30

The World's Best Taxi 32

New! Exclusive! Official!
Stig Merchandise! 34

Jiggled Jaguar 35

RPC vs RPC 36

Top Gear Guide to Spain 38

Supersized Supercar Grid 40

The Stig Reviews Drives... 42

The Best Cars that
Weren't Allowed to Stay
on the Power Laps Board 44

Style Jeremy's Bike 46

Expensive Things
with Bits Missing 48

Comfy and Lovely! 49

Bigger vs Smaller 50

Some Other Things that
Britain is Quite Good At 52

Jeremy's New Favourite:
the McLaren P1 54

Answers 56

INTRODUCTION

Strap in and hang on to your pants, it's going to be a bumpy ride!

Oh, hang on. That's probably not strictly true. How about: do your seatbelt up properly, check your mirrors, indicate clearly and pull away sensibly and safely!

No, that doesn't sound too appealing. OK, last try: welcome to a funny and exciting book about fantastic cars, three men mucking about and a tame racing driver!

Yep, that just about covers it. Let's crack on, eh?

> It's got such a wide range of intoxicating noises!

JEREMY

High point 1: Making sushi for Rachel Riley from *Countdown*. 'Making sushi requires a lot of care. But the results were worth it. Oooh, yes.'

High point 2: Pressing the Sports Exhaust button on the Jaguar F-Type, which makes it even louder.

Low point 1: The scary BAC Mono.

Low point 2: Getting battered by hundreds of tennis balls while demonstrating what it's like to drive the Ferrari F12.

> My bladder's gone! It's completely gone! I've wet myself!

> Come on, little Peugeot, let's see if you can set my trousers on fire!

RICHARD

High point 1: Throwing three hot hatches round the corners of the *TG* test track was a LOT of fun.

High point 2: Getting under a bridge in the HoverVan made him very happy.

High point 3: Driving an Alfa Romeo round an Italian lake looked fantastic.

Low point: Hitting a massive pothole while riding his motorbike. 'I hit a pothole – it was vast. I shot up about fifteen feet in the air off the bike, by the time I was coming back down the bike had hit the opposite wall, it bounced up. Net result, as I was coming down, it leapt up and head-butted me... And it was agony.'

> We did a thing! We did a thing!

James

High point 1: Winning the budget convertible challenge in Spain, though he wasn't that fond of the car he did it in.

'Fairly comprehensive win there for the Audi. So, James May, which of the three cars, knowing what we know now, would you choose to buy?'

'The Ferrari.'

High point 2: Following Jeremy as his caravan disintegrated.

Low point: Sailing in New Zealand, which meant getting a face full of freezing seawater every ten seconds . . . for twelve hours. While being thrown about like a sock in a washing machine.

> I could actually overtake now but this is too amusing! Ha ha haaa!

> This is so catastrophically uncomfortable as a way to travel!

THE STIG

High point 1: Being posted to Spain to drive budget convertibles round the Circuito de Sir Francis Drake.

High point 2: Driving the BAC Mono. Jeremy: 'The second fastest car we've ever had!'

Low point 1: Being left high in the air in a Mazda CX-5 after flipping a caravan on its side.

Low point 2: Being dumped by Jeremy and James. Literally.

Jeremy Reviews...

It's the beating heart of *Top Gear*: a proper review of a brilliant car (or, in this case, two cars). But can you work out which words are missing from Jeremy's quotes?

I have driven the SLS many times and I have never thought, you know what? They should give this thing more [1]. But that's exactly what they've done.

The standard car produces 583 horsepower. This produces 622. And in engineering circles, 622 is known as [2]. It's about that much. And it's got hairs growing out of it.

The upshot is that you can go into a corner fairly confident that you won't come out on the other side all [3]. And that changes the character of the SLS completely.

If you turn the traction control off and stamp on the throttle, you can get it to misbehave. But you sense immediately that it doesn't want to do this. It doesn't like that. 'I am a serious racing car, Englisher! Don't drive with your [4] on!'

Happily, even though it is a serious racing car, Mercedes haven't felt compelled to make the interior as bleak as a Swedish police drama. You still get satnav, and aircon, and many buttons that do... [5].

So it's luxurious, and fast, and very, very good but today it is rather overshadowed... by this.

4

Welcome, everyone, to the world's first electric supercar. I am [6 _____]. It is as quiet as a library for church mice.

You just put it in Sport Plus Mode... and put your foot down. Holy Moley! That is 100mph. 120. 130. 140! This is [7 _____]!

To find out just how fast it is, I lined it up for a drag race against its petrol-powered twin. I can't believe I'll win because under here are 864 batteries.

So this is half a ton heavier. And it's electric, like a [8 _____]. A torch. And how can a glorified torch possibly beat a 6.2-litre V8?

Well, this is what an electric SLS looks like if you take its high-visibility jacket off. And this is the key: the electric motor. Now all electric cars have one of these. But the SLS has four.

It's not a torch! What in the name of God is powering this thing?

This doesn't feel like anything I've ever driven before. It feels [9 _____] and nervous. It feels like a thoroughbred. It feels brilliant.

So let's sum up then. Instant torque, savage power, [10 _____] speed, Mercedes quality, no noise and a petrol bill of exactly... nought.

Fill in the gaps from this list!

mesmerising
gobsmacked
astounded
power
eggy guff
food blender
clown shoes
little hat

mindboggling
tinkle
backwards
things
plopped
twitchy
boring
a lot

5

THE BEST PLACES TO GO FOR A DRIVE... IN THE WORLD

Sometimes Britain can feel like a small and crowded place, but Jeremy has proved there are still beautiful places where you can go for a nice drive. (Though a lot of them are actually abroad.)

IN BRITAIN

'Hertfordshire, 40 miles from London'*

The perfect place to try out the new Ferrari F12 Berlinetta: huge scenery, swooping road, no traffic. Jeremy liked it so much he went back to test the Jaguar F-Type.

The Black Mountains, Wales

Where Jeremy took the Mercedes CLK63 AMG Black in 2008, of course. He wanted somewhere used to monsters and dragons – and eventually, Jeremy decided the mountains were actually named after the car.

FAR AWAY FROM ANYWHERE

Bonneville Salt Flats, USA

Yes, they're in the middle of nowhere. Yes, they're hot and boring. But if you want to drive fast, and get timed doing it, then Bonneville has been the best place in the world for speed freaks since 1912.

Arjeplog, Sweden

Every winter 9,000 engineers visit this tiny remote town to test their cars out in proper winter conditions. The test track is on a frozen lake, where Jeremy had an absolute blast in a Ferrari FF and a Bentley Continental GT.

> I have had more fun than this in my life, I know I have. But I can't quite remember, at the moment, when that was.

*According to Jeremy, anyway. OK, perhaps it was Pitlochry in Scotland. Geography was never our strong point.

NEXT TO WATER

Overseas Highway, Florida Keys

Off the bottom end of Florida are a string of tiny islands, the Florida Keys, joined to the mainland by forty-two bridges. You drive over beautiful blue seas full of dolphins, to sandy beaches lined with palm trees – just don't go in hurricane season.

The Atlantic Road (Atlanterhavsveien), Norway

This 8km stretch of road links eight islands with low swooping bridges, so you feel as if you're flying over the ocean. Watch out for the occasional 80mph winds swiping you sideways.

90 Mile Beach, New Zealand

It's called 90 Mile Beach because it is exactly fifty-five miles long. (No, we don't get it either.) It's a real public road, has spectacular sunsets and some pretty good surfing, apparently. You don't get that on the M4.

UP A HILL

The Troll Ladder (Trollstigen), Norway

One of the most popular tourist destinations in southwest Norway, this twisty road climbs steeply up 2800 feet, with eleven hairpins and a waterfall on the way up to some pretty amazing viewpoints.

The Transfăgărăşan Highway, Romania

Built to give the military a quick route over the mountains in case the Russians invaded, the Transfăgărăşan Highway used 6,000 tons of dynamite and a lot of digging. At the southern end of *Top Gear*'s Best Road is a castle that belonged to Vlad the Impaler... who was the inspiration for Dracula.

AND ONE FAILURE

Blue Ridge Parkway, USA

Americans say the Blue Ridge Parkway in Virginia is simply the best. It's 469 miles long, and very nice to look at. It swoops and curves through beautiful wooded hills. But – and it's a big but – there are speed limits all the way along it, from 20mph to 45mph. So, no thanks. Sorry.

Bye-bye Beeb!

If you've ever watched television, you've probably seen this building: BBC TV Centre in west London.

Loads of shows you know were filmed here – *Blue Peter, Strictly Come Dancing* and *Doctor Who*. Jeremy even drove a Peel P50 through the building.

In 2013 it closed, which meant James could finally hold a proper race through it. So who was quicker: freerunners Tim and Paul, or Dougie the trials bike rider?

Find **two** routes through this maze-like building and work out who got to the finish first (it was Dougie).

START

FINISH

STIG'S FRIDGE

If the Stig had a fridge – which he doesn't – what would it look like?

991

Kwik-Kleen Dry Kleeners

QUAN.	DESCRIPTION	PRICE	AMOUNT
	To clean stains from white overalls: oil, petrol, diesel, custard		£48
	Ditto gloves		£24
	Overnight service 50% surcharge		£36
	Total		£108
	Paid in industrial solvent – many thanks		

NAME

ADDRESS

SOLD BY · CASH · C.O.D. · CHARGE · ON ACCT. · MDSE. RETD. · PAID OUT

DATE

TAX

TOTAL

BAC Mono	1.14.3
Lamborghini Sesto Elemento	1.14.0
Mercedes SLS AMG Black	1.19.0
Mercedes SLS Electric	1.21.7
Peugeot 208 GTi	1.33.2
Renaultsport Clio 200T	1.32.0
Ford Fiesta ST	1.32.7
Mazda CX-5 + caravan	DNF
VW Tiguan + caravan	DNF
Range Rover Sport	1.29.4
VW Golf GTI Mk VII	1.29.6

STIG ON BOARD

I AM THE STIG. NO, REALLY, I AM.

UTTERLY STIGTACULAR!

An A-Z of Top Gear

Because you're never too young to start being a fan. Before you know it you'll be talking about active differentials, flappy paddles and horsepowers!

A is for **Atom** that turns your face funny

B's for **Bugatti** – you'll need LOADS of money

C is for **Camping**. And **Caravans** – yuck!

D's for the bird Stig is baffled by: **Duck**

E is for **E-Type**, this ace car's a Brit

F is for **France**, which Jeremy thinks is . . . beautiful, with excellent roads and food

G is for **Golf GTi** – a hatch that's hot

H is for **Hammond**, who gives all he's got

I is for **India**, where they ate bhaji

J is for **Jeremy** who thinks he's in chaji

K is for Koenigsegeggsegg which we can't spell

L is for Lambo, they're all quick as . . . anything

10

M is for **May**, who's a very clever man

N is for **North Pole**; James wasn't a fan

O is for **Oliver**, Richard's little dear

P is for **Power**, which we like to hear

Q is for **Quiet** like most electric cars

R's for **RPC**, to find out fast stars

S is for **Stig**, whose face can't be found

T is for **Turbo**, which makes a good sound

U is for **Useless**, which the chaps sometimes are

V's for **Vietnam**, where they couldn't buy a car

W is for **W12**. Double V6? You bet!

X is for **X-Bow**, which got Jeremy wet

Y is for **Yugo**, that Jeremy thought crappy

Z is for **Zonda**, that makes Richard happy!

THE NEW BUS FOR LONDON	TEST	FERRARI F12
Very fiddly indeed. It took James fifteen minutes to turn the thing on.	Ease of controls	Fiddly, especially the steering wheel with all the buttons on it.
Smooth as a cloud made of silk. Doesn't accelerate fast enough to make you lose balance.	Ride comfort	Like driving over corrugated metal, all the time. Unless you drive fast, when you're too scared to notice.
The steering is light, but lacks crispness. Visibility is fantastic.	Easy to drive?	Twitchy as a nervous ferret. You need to pay a lot of attention.
It's a pig to reverse, and park.	Easy to manoeuvre?	Not at all bad, for a supercar.
Sixty-two seats, a wheelchair space and room for twenty-five to stand. Plus luggage, shopping and prams.	Capacity	Two people, as long as they're not too 'bonny' and haven't got a lot of luggage.
Pretty good, actually. For a bus. It was designed by Heatherwick Studio, who did the Olympic cauldron.	Appearance	Utterly stunning and drop-dead gorgeous.
It's a hybrid – electric motors turn the wheels, a diesel engine charges the batteries.	Engine	6.3-litre V12 producing 730hp, giving a 0-60mph time of about three seconds.
11.6mpg, which is 40% more efficient than old diesel buses.	Economy	Apparently up to 18mpg.
LED lights, sixteen CCTV cameras, TV screens, regenerative braking, climate-controlled ventilation... lots.	Technology	Electronic differential, F1 traction control, electronic stability control... computer-stuff, basically.
People will stare, and try to get on.	Eye-catching?	People will stare.
4,000,000 people will use it over its lifetime of twelve-fifteen years in London.	Lifetime use	Probably two people will use it for five years and then it'll sit in a museum.
6	SCORE	6

It's close, but if you've got a lot of friends and don't need to get anywhere in a hurry, perhaps the bus is the better vehicle. You could even employ someone to drive it for you. And if the council bought it for you, and parked it in a really big garage, you could get on it whenever you needed it, in return for a small fee.

Nah, who are we kidding? Only joking, of course!

CROSSOVER CARAVAN GAME

Forced to do a proper review of cars suitable for caravanners, James and Jeremy gathered a bunch of fourteen jacked-up diesel hatchbacks with part-time 4WD. Unable to tell them apart, they picked two at random. Play this game the same way!

START Choose your vehicle!
Heads: VW Tiguan.
Tails: Mazda CX-5.

Let's go! Time to do what everyone does in these cars…
Heads: go to the dump.
Tails: wash the car.

Wash the car! Rub-rub-rub. Squeak-squeak-squeak.
Heads: go to the DIY superstore. *Tails:* go to the dump.

Find your car…
Heads: that's the one. Off you go! *Tails:* no, that's a Nissan Kumquat. Try again.

The Dump. Lovely. But have you got enough things to throw away?
Heads: the garden centre. *Tails:* the DIY superstore.

DIY Superstore. Buy some chain and a shovel, for some reason.
Heads: to the dump! *Tails:* to the garden centre!

Try to find your car again…
Heads: you're off! *Tails:* keep trying, it's got to be here somewhere.

The Garden Centre. Buy some bedding plants, or something.
Heads: the dump. *Tails:* watch birds.

The Dump. Again. Gosh, what a lot of rubbish.
Heads: the *TG* track. *Tails:* wash the car.

Finally! You're off for a day of fun.
Heads: the garden centre. *Tails:* wash the car.

Wash the car! Squeak-squeak-squeak. Rub-rub-rub.
Heads: watch birds. *Tails:* go to the dump.

Watch some birds. Then throw your binoculars away.
Heads: time to give the Stig a go! *Tails:* back to the dump.

14

FINISH
Time to cook up a pie and settle down for a comfy night in your caravan. What do you mean, there's nothing left of it?

Hang on, what's this? These trees are very confusing.
Heads: over there looks good. *Tails:* no, this way I think.

Across someone's lawn. Is that your portable toilet behind you?
Heads: get a bit lost. *Tails:* there's the campsite!

Give it some welly! Don't worry about that crunching noise.
Heads: open space ahead! *Tails:* more mud.

Through the mud. Blast through as hard as you can. Don't worry, it's fine.
Heads: through the trees. *Tails:* that looks messy.

Over bits of caravan. Are they yours?
Heads: the end is in site(!) *Tails:* hope they don't mind.

Hook up. Get set. Go! Quick, head off-road for a shortcut.
Heads: zoom off. *Tails:* can you get past?

Got a little scrape. Nothing to worry about.
Heads: through the mud. *Tails:* through the trees.

Through the trees. Ooh, lumpier than you thought. And muddier. Crunch!
Heads: speed up. *Tails:* slow down.

The *TG* Track. Stiggy has a go. This doesn't work.
Heads: you get the VW. *Tails:* you're in the Mazda.

Put some stickers on, and go! Sneak past the Tiguan and take the lead.
Heads: the race is on! *Tails:* watch out!

Floor it! Blimey, that caravan's making a lot of noise. Never mind.
Heads: through the trees. *Tails:* be careful!

Richard Reviews...

It's Richard's turn to dig through the big bag of adjectives and try to come up with a new way of talking about cars. But which words are missing from his review?

Lamborghini Aventador Roadster vs Lamborghini Sesto Elemento

So, er, here we are. Budget car, Lamborghini style. The Aventador Roadster. As you'd expect from Lamborghini, it's basically a roofless wedge of [1]_____ numbers.

Lamborghini's mission has always been to make the best bedroom [2]_____ subjects in the world. Always looking forward. Never back.

I mean look at this thing – it's just pure [3]_____. Everything's dialled up to eleven. Brings out the nine-year-old inside every... forty-year-old. Forty-three. Thirty-eight.

What's really astonishing is that they've been pulling off this trick for fifty years now. That's five decades of unleashing unique [4]_____ machines, each more outrageous than the last.

How do you keep doing extreme... for fifty years? What do you come up with next? Well let's find out what, shall we, because in truth, this isn't the car Lambo rang us about. The car they rang us about makes this look... dull.

Fill in the gaps from this list!

catapults
flabbiness
flamboyant
bumbling
revolutionary
simplicity
oblong

hypercar
wall poster
dazzling
shed
fearsome
theatre
ginormous

It's called the Sesto Elemento, Italian for 'sixth element'. The body is made from a [5] blend of plastic and carbon jointly developed by Lamborghini and Boeing.

Such an extreme car deserves an extreme location. Which is why we've returned to the [6] Imola race track. Let's give it a shot... Woah! It's different! It's superbike fast! God, it nearly wheelies!

But what I love is they've done all this brutal [7] and weight-saving in an Italian way, it's... beautiful. This central spar looks like it belongs in a modern art gallery.

I think Lamborghini has learnt from Porsche the art of charging more for less. So this thing, with its missing dashboard and seats, is... wait for it... £1.95 million!

However, there's no time to be shocked by that, because right now I'm in a £2 million [8] and I've got Imola all to myself. Because it's light, you can brake so late...

...and because it's light, it can turn so hard without trying to tear its own tyres off. And because it's light, when you get out of the turn, the 570 horsepower V10 just [9] it.

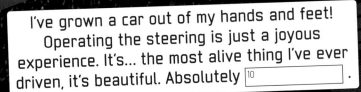

I've grown a car out of my hands and feet! Operating the steering is just a joyous experience. It's... the most alive thing I've ever driven, it's beautiful. Absolutely [10] .

And when you've finished, you can get out and remind yourself that you've been driving something that looks... like this.

HOW TO HOLD AN ALL-STAR CELEBRITY SUMMER BARBECUE FESTIVAL EVENT

When a new Reasonably Priced Car joins the show, you need to get a bunch of times on the board all at once, or it looks a bit bare. What's the solution?

All the way back in 2006, when the Lacetti became the RPC, Jeremy and Richard held a drop-in coffee morning, but they didn't make a lot of effort: one table, six chairs, some biscuits and two sorts of jam. By the time the Cee apostrophe D replaced the Lacetti in 2010, they'd classed up their act no end. Really pushed the boat out. So they knew what to get when the Vauxhall Astra Tech Line arrived.

CATERING

- Nibbles – peanuts, crisps in several flavours, little cheesy biscuits, twig-shaped things
- Fondant fancies on a cake stand. Classy
- Posh biscuits that come in a box
- Battenburg *and* Swiss Roll
- Thirty-two sausages (more than enough)
- Burgers – don't waste money. Once they're cooked by Richard no one will be able to tell if it's a burger or a lump of charcoal
- A cauliflower (in case you get a vegetarian)
- Tea bags and instant coffee
- Little sugar packets and tubs of milk
- Paper plates, paper napkins and polystyrene cups
- Red sauce *and* brown sauce (in case anyone is from Up North)
- Lots of bags of value bread (to raise the seat for shorter guests)

HOSPITALITY

- A marquee, because it's going to rain. Maybe you could get a gazebo, whatever that is
- Those white plastic garden chairs that must breed in the night because they're EVERYWHERE ON THE PLANET
- Loungers, in case you need to do small talk

ENTERTAINMENT

- A drum kit, keyboards and guitars. *Top Gear* likes musicians, especially from the 1970s when Jeremy and James were young
- Fairground sideshows – a punchy boxing thing, a bouncy castle, a spinning sheep ride... whatever you fancy!
- Exercise equipment – hey, you never know. One time they had a Power Plate machine, which wiggles about as you stand on it

DOS AND DONTS

- Do aim high. Eventually, Harrison Ford, Johnny Depp and Angelina Jolie *will* turn up, if you're persistent. Probably.
- Do send out the invites early. Celebrities are busy people. They need *at least* a week's notice.
- Do try to remember everyone's name. Jeremy had to call one person 'Well Spoken Man' at the Lacetti coffee morning.
- Do show some interest occasionally in people's driving. At the very least, keep an eye out that they're not about to skid off the track and hit you.
- Don't monopolize the guests you are attracted to, and ignore the others.

SAFETY EQUIPMENT

- Helmets for everyone in a range of sizes
- Some cones and that stripy yellow and black tape
- A man in a high-visibility waistcoat with a fire extinguisher
- A map of the track

OTHER

- Name badges for everyone you've invited
- A tame racing driver
- A Reasonably Priced Car. Bring plenty of spares: tyres, clutches, mirrors, bumpers... actually, to be on the safe side, bring a couple of spare cars

Top Gear JUDGE THINGS

The *Top Gear* presenters have always had strong opinions on motoring-related things. As His Honour Justice Clarkson once said: 'The world just doesn't work without us in it, does it?'

Motorway service station trousers

What really bothers me is why do they sell trousers? I've never got halfway down a motorway and thought, 'I forgot my trousers! I'd better get these elasticated-waist beige ones.'

BAD!

The M4

I have to spend a lot of time on it, and it's *awful*.

If you think the M4 is the worst motorway in the world, why do you spend all your life driving up and down it?

BAD!

Formula 1 rules

James: 'Surely it should be the pinnacle of automotive technology... active aerodynamics, traction control, ABS, invisibility cloaks, they should be able to have anything they want.'

Jeremy: 'The problem is the organisers are trying to make Formula 1 a level playing field, to make it a driver's championship, but it isn't. You could put Sebastian Vettel in a Marussia – he's gonna come last.'

'Exactly, let's just make it a championship for carmakers, and let the designers have completely free reign. They can do anything.'

BAD!

Vehicle electronics, especially voice activation

It *never* works. When it first came out, voice activation was just for the radio or satnav. Now it's for every single feature on the car and in your life. And it has to understand every accent. It just can't cope. You're driving along, and say 'Radio Two.'

'Accessing bank account. Transferring funds.'

'God, no!'

TopGear
TECHNOLOGY
CENTRE

BAD!

Sports Mode

Stig did a *TG* lap in the new Golf GTI set in Normal Mode: 1.29.6, which is pretty good. Then he did another lap in Sports Mode, which beefed up the suspension, and the front differential, quickened the throttle response and made the steering heavier. His time? Exactly the same, 1.29.6. And in Comfort Mode, which makes it all soft and gooey? Pretty much the same: 1.29.5.

All the knobs and buttons for the lights and the wipers and the indicators are all on the steering wheel which moves about, so they're never where you left them. You can't even sneeze in this car.

BAD!

Steering wheels with all the controls on

BAD!

It shouldn't say Sport, it should just say Worse.

BAD!

Classic British motorcar stamps

Lotus Esprit, fine. Aston Martin DB5, fine. MG MGB... so-so. Ford Anglia 105E police car? NO! Morris Minor Post Office Van? NO again! 'That's more dreadful heritage Britain nonsense,' said James.

A VW Golf is £4,000 less expensive than a Tiguan, so I'd buy one of those. Then I'd take the £4,000 that I'd saved to the tip, and throw it away. No, I'd spend the £4,000 on a fortnight's holiday in the South of France... in a hotel.

BAD!

VW Tiguan

New hybrid supercars from McLaren, Porsche and Ferrari

 But that's another story!

HOW TO BUILD A HOVERVAN

We get a lot of rain in Britain. But there isn't a vehicle that can drive on normal roads but also cope with a sudden flood, which can hide obstacles like signs, bins and cows. Until now!

> Richard Hammond – engage Hover Mode! We are rising! Engage Thrust Mode!

Jeremy thought you could put wheels on a hovercraft, but Richard said that wouldn't work. 'Or, this is my other plan,' replied Jeremy, 'we get a car, and turn it into a hovercraft.' James thought he might be onto something, but it would need to be big enough to fit more engines in.

To get the work done quickly, the chaps had a quick montage, with inspirational music. In no time at all, they had the HoverVan Mk I ready for its first test drive.

> What I think is critical, is that 364 days of the year, this has to just be a car. And it's absolutely perfect at that.

To test it for that important other 'soggy' day, they found a handy reservoir, converted to Hover Mode and donned attractive outfits.

> It's quite exciting. I can't walk.

Oh dear. Not enough **POWER**.

SO... back to the Top Secret Engineering Centre, where Richard replaced the two 90hp engines with 600hp of superbike and track car goodness. James upgraded the rubber skirts.

> I've also added these inflatable rubber tubes to make it a bit less sinky.

Fire up the lift engine! Fire up the thrust engine!

I love all the things we have to say!

They were so confident the HoverVan Mk II would work, they wore their own clothes and headed for the River Avon. On the plus side, it worked. On the minus side, they hit the bank straight away. Jeremy said it wasn't his fault.

He was soon proved right, when they found a lock. They went a bit sinky again, and Richard got damp. 'Here's what we must do,' said Jeremy. 'We must get it out of the lock. And then we'll get a tow. And then we can edit all of this out.'

In my defence, hovercrafts have no brakes, no reverse, extremely haphazard steering, and if you cut the lift engine, it can't be restarted on water.

I'm the wettest a man has ever been!

They pressed on, only to meet the biggest challenge yet: a weir. Going down was actually fine. Going up was... not.

They stopped to refuel the two-gallon tank, and headed for Tewkesbury, which often floods. Locals were a bit surprised at the noise, and the spray, which made them... a few enemies. Richard summed it up: 'The thing with hovercrafting is, it's brilliant, brilliant, brilliant – disaster.'

AAAARRGH!

Sorry! Sorry!

On balance then, apart from the noise, the spray, the terrible danger, impracticality, unreliability, total uncontrollability, catastrophic fuel consumption, terrible expense and disastrous damage caused, it was a *total* success.
Well done, chaps.

This is literally my idea of heaven!

the Burmese lorrying test

Burma poses some special challenges for the long-distance lorry driver. Find out if you are up to the job with this rigorous test.

Between India and Thailand is a big beautiful country called The Republic of the Union of Myanmar, though loads of people (and Jeremy) still call it by its old name, Burma. The British decided they were in charge there for about seventy years, which didn't work out too well. Then World War II came along and frankly, that was a total nightmare. After that, the country was under the thumb of a general who was (to put it gently) utterly bonkers.

Things are getting better now, and Burma needs help to move things around this huge, mountainous country. Could you do a bit of long-distance lorry driving?

WHAT KIND OF LORRY HAVE YOU GOT?

a) A 2,300-watt sound system, with huge speakers. Oh, and some kind of big old lorry to put it in, made by Isuzu or Mitsubishi, in 1959 or 1976. What, the back tips up? Why?

b) A crane and two winches, with hydraulic legs and lots of exciting levers. Shame the lorry is utterly knackered.

c) An extensively modified and MASSIVE proper lorry... with a wooden bench for a seat.

We had to bring lorries, mate. That's a van.

There are gauges... nothing works. Not one of them.

WHAT SHOULD A LORRY DRIVER WEAR?

a) A shirt and tie. Modern lorry drivers are crisp and sharp.

b) What? Same as I always wear. Check shirt, jeans, and a bandana for my flowing locks.

c) Vest! With egg stains! Shorts! Big boots! Chunky chocolate bars!

NOTE: Burmese traffic drives on the right. In right-hand drive vehicles. This means bus passengers get off in the middle of the road. Get used to it.

HOW GOOD IS YOUR SENSE OF DIRECTION?

a) I decide the general plan then leave the boring details to someone else.

b) I always end up getting blamed, but these signs are very confusing.

c) Are we there yet?

DO YOU GET ON WELL WITH PEOPLE?

a) Of course! Talk loudly and confidently, then wave bundles of money. Everyone likes me.

b) Sorry. Sorry. Sorry. Gosh, they're so nice.

c) Whoops!

ARE THERE ANY PHYSICAL ISSUES THAT COULD AFFECT YOUR LORRYING?

a) I'm in agony. The endless gear changes and savage brakes have knackered my left knee.

b) Just my bad temper at the appalling quality of my lorry and the behaviour of my colleagues.

c) Numb bum. And a horse kicked my wrist.

> I'm not a young man, and I'm not a fit man.

> Ow. I'm sitting on a church pew!

TEST YOUR NIGHT VISION: WHAT CAN YOU SEE?

a) Is that a moped with no lights on? My headlights are glowworms in jamjars.

b) Aah, a dog. Crikey, a huge truck!

c) Nothing. Just my own stupid reflection in my windscreen.

SOME ROADS ARE STEEP, POORLY MAINTAINED OR UNDERWATER. WILL YOU COPE?

a) Loading my truck with bricks to make it comfier means I can only crawl uphill. But getting across rivers is easy thanks to POWER.

b) Oh no! My little truck keeps getting stuck on something. Help!

c) I'll give you a shove...

> I thought we were stuck behind a moped!

> You're a right dipstick!

> This is my new top speed.

> RAMMING!

CAN YOU DO YOUR OWN REPAIRS?

a) I've got a hammer. Can you do anything with that?

b) I am extremely practical, which is crucial with this rotten box of junk.

c) Nothing serious broke... apart from the stupid exhausts I added.

BURMESE DRIVERS ARE POLITE AND HELPFUL. ARE YOU?

a) I had to dump all those bricks and that massive tree root on the road. Someone else can clear them up.

b) If you want something lifted with a crane, I'm your man. Unless it breaks. Which it definitely will.

c) If you break down, you're on your own. Sorry, mate.

ACCOMMODATION IN RURAL AREAS MAY BE... BASIC. HOW WILL YOU COPE?

a) Not well, so I put a proper bed in the back.

b) Not well, so I hung a climbers' tent off my crane.

c) Not well, so I built a spacious villa with a terrace, kitchen, wardrobe and shower in the back of my lorry.

> Clarkson! Very funny. I don't like heights.

> I don't like snoring.

WARNING: Do not attempt to substitute horses for lorries. It will all end in pain.

> Ow! Ow! Ow! My nadgers are getting a pummelling!

> Ha haa! I'm terrified!

BURMESE TRUCKS ARE OFTEN MODIFIED. WHAT WOULD YOU DO TO YOUR VEHICLE?

a) Make it into a convertible Sports Lorry!

b) Make it high-vis, safe and comfortable!

c) Make it EVEN BIGGER! Oh, and slower.

> Not all of my improvements have turned out to be improvements.

RESULTS

Mostly As: Your leadership and driving skills are admirable, but a bit more consideration for others would help.

Mostly Bs: Your practical skills will be invaluable. Shame you have such poor taste in vehicles.

Mostly Cs: Think less about how your lorry looks and more about how it performs!

MATCH THE OUTBURST

Over 160 celebrities have sat in a Reasonably Priced Car. Some were concentrating too hard to say anything, but the rest felt the need to yell something. Can you match the quote to the celebrity?

A Bill Bailey, comedian

B Amy Williams, ex-Olympic athlete

C Jimmy Carr, comedian

D Joss Stone, musician

E Warwick Davis, actor

F Rachel Riley from *Countdown*

G Al Murray, comedian

H Johnny Vaughan, presenter

1. Turn, turn, turn, ya doughnut!

2. Don't lose your bottle! Keep your foot down!

3. OK, here we go. Skeleton run, but in a car.

4. I think I might have broken the car...

5. Ooh, can't get it in gear.

6. Into fifth... give it some more welly...

7. Was that a crow? Or a raven?

8. Come on, reasonably priced car!

A: ....   D: ....   G: ....
B: ....   E: ....   H: ....
C: ....   F: ....

29

James Reviews...

Jeremy was never going to do this one, because he thinks Porsche 911s have stayed exactly the same for fifty years. So James did the honours – but which words are missing from his review?

In truth though, this is all new. The body, for example, is now made from [2] which means it's much lighter, and lighter is good. The 3.8-litre flat-6 engine has been upgraded. And all-new suspension, which does its job [3] .

It's changed rather less over the last fifty years than I have. The interior may be more ordered, and Porsche [1] will spot that it's a couple of inches longer. But to normal people it looks like just another 911.

For fifty years Porsche have bloody-mindedly stuck with this daft idea of building a car with the engine at the back but, half a century of consistent fiddling around, and they've made it work brilliantly.

It's so good that it brought on a temporary attack of [4] . Turn in, give it a little squeeze of power... feel it all tighten up. How could you not like a 911?

Strange to say it but this car has a big problem. And that problem is classic 911 [5] . To them this car is the work of Satan, and simply because it isn't an old 911.

The engine is another 911 classic 3.8-litre flat-6, and develops 360 horsepower... and a lovely buzz. Gets you in there. And although the body may look like it's come from a 1960s Porsche, almost all of it has been remodelled in [6]_____.

What they actually want in a new 911 is a 911 that's new... and yet not new. What they want... is this. This looks like an old 911. But the whole car is custom-built. And where necessary, it's [7]_____ with modern touches.

The precision of the steering... you didn't feel that, obviously, because you're not in here, but it's utterly intuitive. Look, it's an old 911, it feels old, and then I get to the Hammerhead and the brakes are [8]_____.

They could have overdone this. It would be possible to put the turbo engine in this car. They could have made it [9]_____ powerful, but they haven't. They've concentrated on the sensation of performance: the noise, the vibration, the feel of the steering. That's what actually matters.

Before we go any further, you're probably wondering what all this [10]_____ costs. Well, the bottom line is: it's a lot. Around £280,000, in fact.

Fill in the gaps from this list!

bobble
impeccably
nostril
peppered
carbon fibre
nerds
tremendous
wangle

yobbishness
blubber
ludicrously
excellence
aluminium
pork pie
enthusiasts
throbbing

The Competitors

Britain: 1997 Fairway Driver black cab with only 320,000 miles on the clock.

Mexico: 1970 VW Beetle from Mexico City, where there are 50,000 of them.

USA: Ford Crown Victoria from New York, with a 4.6-litre V8 capable of 130mph... once

India: Hindustan Ambassador. Underneath it's a Morris Oxford, which was old-fashioned half a century ago.

South Africa: Toyota Hiace, where they're feared for their wild aggression.

Germany: Mercedes E-Class. Tidy, clean and reliable. Of course.

Russia: Stretched Lincoln Town Car. They really are used as taxis by rich Russians. It's not just because it'll be funny.

The World's Best Taxi

START

Everybody passes the black cab!

Stretch limo spins out, New York cab breaks it in two and then collapses!

Black cab knocks a door off the VW!

FINISH

...but Richard gets passed by the Hiace, the VW, and the Ambassador, which wins and is officially the best taxi!*

Much good-natured jostling!

Merc shunts the black cab, speeding it up for a bit!

*Not really, it's still the London black cab, whatever anyone else says.

What's the best taxi? Easy – the London black cab. It's world famous, and been around forever. But other countries would say it's slow and uncomfortable. There is only one way to find out the truth: in the prism of the furnace through the looking glass of the crucible of motorsport. Let's race!

That plywood cab office looks perilously close to the track. I sincerely hope no harm befalls it.

Hiace veers everywhere, clouting everyone!

Hiace pushes Merc off the track in a somersault!

Russian limo slides wildly round corners!

There is the finishing line. I think I could win this!

Black cab cheats again and is in sight of the finish...

Other taxis force Richard to go *through* the cab office!

Black cab is outpaced on the hills... straights... and turns – but takes a shortcut!

New! Exclusive! Official!*
Stig Merchandise!

In response to overwhelming demand (not really) *Top Gear* is overjoyed to announce a stunning range of exquisite exclusive objects inspired by our tame racing driver. Hey, if carmakers can try and sell us soap and handbags... why not?

Food!

Pets!

Games!

Safety!

Vehicles!

Occasionwear!

Things!

Plants!

Available at all good retailers now!**

Jiggled Jaguar

Work out how to rearrange these squares so they make a lovely picture of the Jaguar F-Type. You could cut them out, but that would be cheating.

I think this is one of the best-looking cars ever made.

Fill the numbers into this grid in the right place.

RPC vs RPC

So we're now on the fourth Reasonably Priced Car. They get pushed pretty hard, these frankly unremarkable four-door boxes on wheels. How do they compare?

SUZUKI LIANA

£9,995 in 2002 – *very* reasonably priced. This one did over 1,600 laps of the *TG* track, and got through 400 tyres, 400 brake pads, six clutches, two gear linkages and a wing mirror. Lionel Richie and Trevor Eve snapped off a front wheel, David Soul knackered two gearboxes in one day and Patrick Kielty snapped the front suspension.

Driven by: Seventy-six people, including eleven F1 drivers

Fastest F1 time: 1.42.9, Lewis Hamilton (on his second visit)

Fastest non-F1 time: 1.46.7, Ellen MacArthur

Slowest time: 2.06.0, Richard Whiteley (slower than blind veteran Billy Baxter)

Mark Webber came back in 2013 but couldn't beat Lewis Hamilton's time

CHEVROLET LACETTI

£10,000 in 2006. Had a 1.8-litre engine producing 119hp, giving a 0-60mph time of 9.5secs and a top speed of 121mph. In 2010 it was given a Viking burial under a chimney, which came down on the Lacetti like a ton of bricks. Because it was a ton of bricks.

Driven by: Fifty-seven people

Fastest time: 1.45.83, Jay Kay

Slowest time: 2.08.9, Jimmy Carr (spun off)

KIA CEE APOSTROPHE D

£14,000 in 2010 – quite a big jump in reasonableness. Had a 1.6-litre engine producing 124hp, which meant a top speed of 119mph. This was clearly the fastest RPC on the track, with sixteen celebs beating the Lacetti's fastest time, and nineteen of them beating the Liana. Matt LeBlanc and Rowan Atkinson were faster in this car than *all* the F1 drivers in the Liana.

Driven by: Forty-one people

Fastest time: 1.42.1, Matt LeBlanc

Slowest time: 2.09.1, Damian Lewis (in the snow)

> What a machine it is! It can go from 0 to 60 in a dazzling 10.4 seconds.

Charles Dance goes sideways

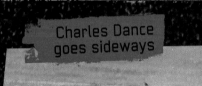

VAUXHALL ASTRA TECH LINE

£17,345 in 2013. Is that really reasonable? Though the price does include a Lifetime Warranty. Has a 1.6-litre engine giving only 113hp, so 0-60mph takes 10.9secs and the top speed is 118mph.

Driven by: Seventeen people so far

Fastest time*: 1.44.7, Aaron Paul

Slowest time*: 1.54.5, Jack Whitehall (though he didn't know how to drive!)

Warwick Davis sits on some bread

* May have changed by the time you read this, obviously.

TOP GEAR GUIDE TO SPAIN

Spain has had a few problems recently, so is it still worth going there for a driving holiday? Here's what you might find.

Spain is sunny. You want a convertible, and it makes sense in these cash-strapped times to go for a budget version. So Richard chose the second-cheapest Ferrari: £198,000 of Ferrari 458 Spider. Jeremy picked the even-cheaper McLaren MP4-12C Spider, at only £195,000. James did it properly, and actually went for proper value with the Audi R8 V10 Spyder – only £121,000. What a bargain!

Bits of Spain are very rich. Puerto Banus is full of holidaying millionaires and their orange girlfriends, the type of people who are not at all impressed by grey Audis... but massively impressed by gold-flake yellow convertibles. James's Audi got photographed twenty-two times going round the harbour; Richard's Ferrari, forty-seven times; and Jeremy's McLaren... four hundred and thirty-eight times.

Bits of Spain are quiet. That makes it the perfect place to test how loud your cheap car can get. For instance, the Audi produced 105db; the McLaren 105db; and the Ferrari 107db. And there are no locals about to complain.

This is what the McLaren was always meant to be: open top. You really, really want this.

Parts of Spain are mountainous. The Sierra Nevada Mountains have the highest road in Europe, and are brilliant to drive through, especially if you can't afford a roof. They drove happily up to 2,000 metres where there was still snow and then – ah. The road ran out.

There are only three cars on this motorway, and we're in all of them!

The roads are peaceful. Watch out for goats, though.

The infrastructure is impressive. Spain has a completely deserted spare airport, Ciudad Real, doing nothing, just in case they need it later. This is massively useful if you want to do a speed test in your cheap cars. Richard hit 193mph, James said 'buffeting!' and made it to 186mph. Jeremy in the McLaren got up to 198mph! 'Victory, therefore, is mine!' James then came up with a twist: start with the roofs down, but finish with them up. Unlike the others, Richard couldn't move while his roof was going up. So in this version, he was slower than the Audi.

THE OTHER SPANISH TRIPS

2005 Richard got chased by bulls in Pamplona, and then drove a Lamborghini Murcielago to see which was scarier. Or something.

2007 The team visited the Stig's favourite holiday resort to see if anything could compete with the BMW M3. It couldn't.

There's lots of space. There's enough unused housing estate on the outskirts of Madrid to build your own race circuit. If you have your own tame racing driver, why not get him posted out to set a target lap in a Jaguar XKR-S convertible? Just watch out for speed humps. Richard was a second behind the Stig's time, with Jeremy half a second behind him and James another second slower.

2010 Jeremy took the BMW X5 to Spain to see if it drove any differently on Spanish roads. It didn't.

SUPERSIZED SUPERCAR GRID

There may not be that many of them made, but there are hundreds of different super-fast, super-gorgeous and super-pricey supercars. Can you slot this tasty selection into the right places in the grid opposite?

To get you started, some words can only fit in one position!

6 letters
FORD GT

7 letters
BAC MONO

8 letters
SPYKER C8
LEXUS LFA

9 letters
ASCARI A10
NOBLE M600
AUDI R8 V10
FERRARI FF
NISSAN GTR

11 letters
LOTUS ESPRIT

12 letters
MASERATI MC12
ARIEL ATOM 500
PAGANI HUAYRA

13 letters
MCLAREN MP412C
GUMPERT APOLLO

14 letters
HENNESSEY VENOM

15 letters
KOENIGSEGG AGERA
SSC ULTIMATE AERO

16 letters
PORSCHE CARRERA GT
ASTON MARTIN ONE 77

20 letters
BENTLEY CONTINENTAL GT

22 letters
MERCEDES BENZ SLR MCLAREN

23 letters
BUGATTI VEYRON SUPERSPORT

24 letters
LAMBORGHINI SESTO ELEMENTO

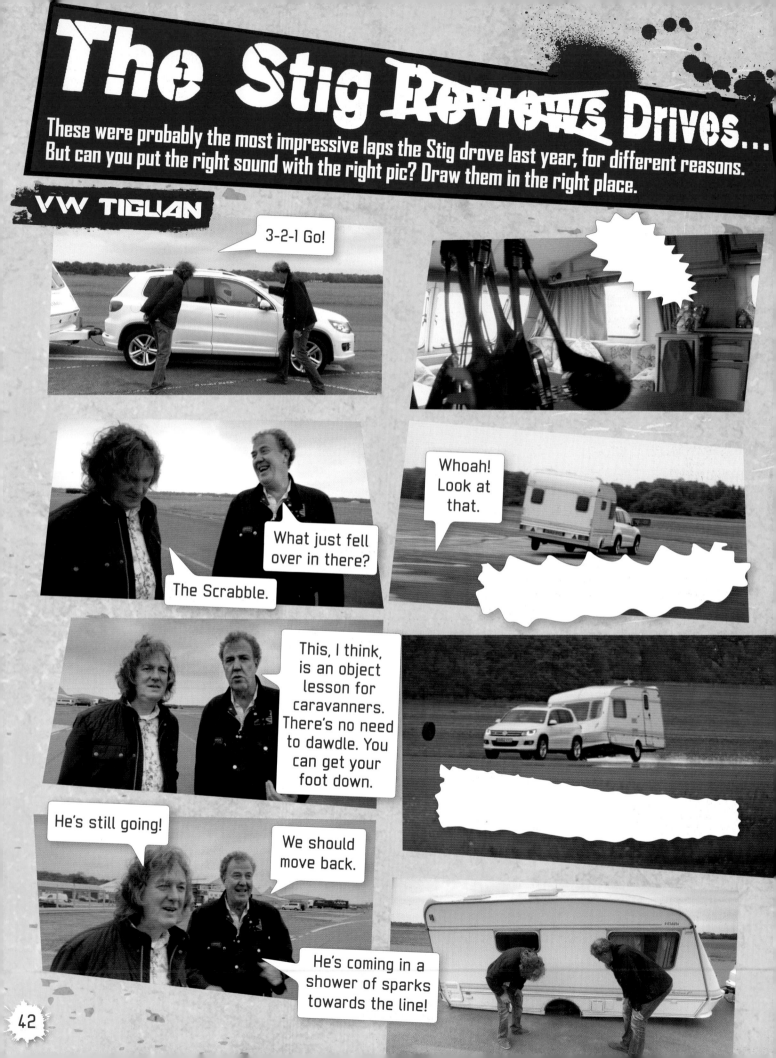

MAZDA CX5

3-2-1 Go!

Ooh! Smoke *pouring* off the brakes!

BAC MONO

Stig snaps to attention and he's off! Flicking off the line like a flea.

No stereo, of course, just the sound of that Cosworth-tuned engine.

Stig is brave, even on the brink of a crisis!

And across the line!

Choose from these sounds:
Squeeeeee!
RRRRRRRRUURRNN...
SKRRREEE-whump!
Splomph!
KDUNK-KSSSSHHH
NEEEyooowww
SqueeAARGH-frunnk-fudunk!
Wah-wah-waaaahh...
VNNNN! VRRRNG!
BRRINNG!
Clatter-dunk-tsh!
RRAAAARRRRGH!
poot
KTSSH!

43

THE BEST CARS that weren't allowed to stay on the POWER LAPS BOARD

Top Gear has strict rules. For a car to stay on the Power Laps Board, it has to be a proper car that you can buy and drive on the public road... and get over a speed hump.

Renault R24 F1 car — 0.59.0

Well, obviously this doesn't qualify: it has no windscreen wipers, or a number plate, or indicators. But it is a real, proper F1 car, which can go from 0mph to 125mph *and back to zero again* in just seven seconds! No other car has come close to getting round the *TG* track in under a minute... yet.

> I don't like this. No, no, no. No, I don't want this.

> This is Stig's birthday and Christmas present all rolled into one!

Lotus T125 — 1.03.8

A track-day car inspired by F1 but with a bit more room in the cockpit, and which doesn't need sixteen highly trained engineers with several million pounds-worth of kit just to get the engine started. Jeremy was terrified!

> This car is fantastic. It's an extraordinary example of what can be done when there are no rules.

Aston Martin DBR9 — 1.08.6

This is a proper racing car, based on the DB9 that you can drive on the road. Because it's made of carbon fibre, it weighs a ton less than the road car. Its V12 chucks out 600hp, and it can do 0-60mph in 3.4secs. And the front of it looks angry. Grrr.

Pagani Zonda R — 1.08.5

This one's insane (obviously, it's a Pagani). It's illegal for racing or driving on the road, plus it's too noisy to be driven on most British racetracks, so you'd need your own private track. Quite an expensive toy, then. But it can do 0-60mph in three seconds, and lap the Nürburgring in 6mins 40secs!

Caparo T1   1.10.6

The first realistic attempt to make a F1-style car that you can legally drive on the road. It has indicators, and a passenger seat. And a 3.5-litre V8 engine delivering 575hp. It weighs so little that the power-to-weight ratio is twice that of a Veyron, and can do 0-60mph in 2.5secs. Jeremy was excited. You would have to be very rich, very fit, and very brave to buy this car.

God almighty! You can forget Enzos! You can forget Koenigseggs! This is in a different league!

Ferrari FXX   1.10.7

Based on the Enzo, but with a bigger engine, you don't get to just drive the FXX: you have to say which track you want to play at, and Ferrari take it there for you, and then take it back to the factory afterwards.

Hahaa! Woah! That moment when it turns in, it changes direction – it turns like a swallow!

Lamborghini Sesto Elemento   1.14.0

It's almost entirely made of carbon and plastic, and looks like an evil spaceship. The bendy windscreen isn't glass, because that would be too heavy. For a mere £1.95 million you get a 570hp, 5.2-litre V10 engine in a car weighing under a ton, which means you can do 0-60mph in 2.5secs. Richard loved it. What a shame you'll never see one on the road.

45

STYLE JEREMY'S BIKE

Amazingly, Jeremy has bought a two-wheeled vehicle. Even more astonishingly, it hasn't got a motor!

MOTORISTS THANK YOU FOR LETTING ME USE YOUR ROADS

Yes, Jeremy has bought a bicycle of some kind. It's done wonders for his core strength, whatever that is. Richard couldn't believe Jeremy didn't know what kind of bike he'd got. 'Is the front wheel a lot bigger than the back wheel?'

'No! They're all the same!'

'Does it have two little ones at the back?' asked James.

jet engine?

A bike is slow, quiet and cheap, unlike Jeremy's usual preferred modes of transport. To make up for these failings, it should at least be stylishly unique. Get out your crayons and design a bike (and accessories) worthy of Mr Clarkson.

adjustable wing?

Ooh bump! BUMP! Really bumpy here. This is deeply uncomfortable now. Ooh! OW!

front spoiler?

computer-controlled suspension?

racing slicks?

EXPENSIVE THINGS WITH BITS MISSING

As *Top Gear* has proved often, car makers charge more for cars which have had parts taken off them – supposedly to make them lighter, and therefore faster. These things have all been made much more expensive – but can you work out what's been removed?

was £1million NOW JUST £2 million!

was £30 NOW ONLY £55!

was £300 billion NOW ONLY £450 billion!

was £300 NOW JUST £425!

was £799 NOW ONLY £1049!

was $45 million NOW JUST $62 million!

was £650,000 NOW JUST £1.5 million!

was £300 million NOW JUST £545 million!

Comfy and Lovely!

The population of Britain is getting older, but modern cars are not designed for the elderly. They have too many buttons and screens saying incomprehensible things, the ride is too harsh, the seats are all wrong... But worry no more. New from *TG*: the **Rover James!**

> Ooh, that's nice. I said, THAT'S NICE. Isn't it? Yes. That's nice.

Y522 XGJ

Features:
- Painted the lovely colour of a hearing aid
- Pet cage on the roof*
- Speedo that only goes up to 20mph**
- Nice big mirrors
- Simple clear dashboard
- Reversing aids including lovely explosive airbags for safety***
- Enhanced squidgy bumpers
- Squeaky ball under the brake, so you know when you're pressing the right pedal
- Radio that only plays the theme tune from *The Horse of the Year Show*****
- Satnav directing you to only four places, with a lovely old man's voice
- Nice high seats, which are lovely
- Tow hitch that can tow a shopping trolley
- 'Back-to-car' technology to help you find your car again in a car park
- Upholstery that sheds liquid*****

> You idiot!

> What?

> Well it's ruined!

> Yes but it can't go on the motorway going the wrong way.

> No, we can't go *anywhere*, because you exploded the car!

* This has compromised the waterproofing slightly, but what's the point of moaning about the weather?

** At which point it's actually doing 115mph, and your cat may fly off the roof.

*** Watch out for heart attacks.

**** Warning: causes uncontrollable clapping.

***** Just in case of little accidents. Like when you explode the car approaching a motorway from the wrong direction.

BIGGER VS smaller

> It feels like I'm driving a luxury hotel room through a swamp!

Jeremy thinks bigger things are better, like the old Range Rover Sport. Richard prefers smaller things, like the new Range Rover Sport. Who's right? You decide! Vote for your favourite in each of these categories.

Richard was properly impressed with the new Range Rover Sport. It could cope with hills and mud and water and bumps. And on the track it could hold its head up high, thanks to over 500hp and being half a ton lighter than the old Range Rover. But Jeremy likes being able to sit down on the tailgate of the big old Sport when he goes for a walk.

> Bigger, as we know, is always better than smaller.

> Well... not always. Not in bruises, it's not.

Hair

Cheryl Cole ☐ *or* ☐ Harry Hill?

House

Mansion ☐ *or* ☐ Tent?

Shoes

Platform heels ☐ *or* ☐ Flip flops?

Pocket money

Enough to buy a footballer ☐ or ☐ Enough to buy a football?

Dog

Great Dane ☐ or ☐ Miniature Schnauzer?

Musician

Mick Fleetwood ☐ or ☐ Kylie?

Sandwich

Double-triple decker ☐ or ☐ Diet sarnie?

Telly

60-inch widescreen ☐ or ☐ Little portable?

Mobile phone

1980s mobile ☐ or ☐ Modern smartphone?

Injury

Broken leg ☐ or ☐ Paper cut on finger?

Tot up the ticks, and your winner is…

BIG THINGS ☐ or ☐ small things

Some Other Things that Britain is Quite Good At

Top Gear makes British cars, like the Hammerhead Thrust iEagle, the HoverVan and the P45. But does anyone else? Yes, they do. Lots of them. And that's not the only thing we should be really proud of.

The NHS is the best rated health system in the world

2013: 1.5 million cars built 2.5 million engines built

310,837 Nissan Kumquats built in 2013

2013 Tour de France winner

4.7 billion people worldwide watch Premier League football

450 million Harry Potter books sold

1 in 3 Fords sold anywhere in the world has a British-made **engine**

2012 Olympics: **29 gold** **17 bronze** **19 silver**

This feels a bit special, this does.

Britain has the safest roads in the world

£27 billion in automotive exports

Cambridge University is the 4th best rated university in the world

British music industry is worth £3.5billion (largely because of One Direction, Adele and Coldplay)

Alan Sugar Richard Branson Simon Cowell

London cabbies are the best trained in the world

Fish and chips Full English breakfast Chicken tikka masala Pork pie 300+ kinds of cheese

720,000 workers depend on automotive industries

32 million tourists spend **£18 billion** here every year

The BBC – all of it – but especially a little TV show called *Top Gear!*

Jeremy's New Favourite: the McLaren P1

Jeremy went to interesting Belgium to test a new challenger to the famous G-Wiz: a clever little hybrid from McLaren called the P1.

Like many other new supercars, the P1 is missing a lot of little luxuries like, er, carpets, paint and glass. To make up for what's missing, it has 324 batteries producing 176 horsepower, which run an electric motor.

And to *really* put a smile on Jeremy's face, it also has a 3.8-litre V8 petrol engine with two turbos, which top up those batteries... with another 722 horsepower.

Depending on where you are – town, motorway, mountain or track – the P1 changes shape. It squats down, stiffens up and twitches its wing about... all to make the air slide over the car better, or push it down more, or suck it forwards. This is very, very clever British engineering.

This car weighs less than a Vauxhall Astra. That of course makes it economical. And fast. *Really* fast. *Mind-blowingly* fast.

The throttle is a hyperspace button. Step on it... and you're gone.

'For years, cars have all been basically the same, but this really isn't. It's a game-changer, a genuinely new chapter in the history of motoring. In town, it's as eco-friendly as a health food shop. On a motorway it's comfortable, and produces no more carbon dioxide than a family saloon. And on a track, it can rip a hole through time.'

ANSWERS

Page 4: Jeremy Reviews...

1) power, 2) a lot, 3) backwards, 4) clown shoes,
5) things, 6) astounded, 7) mindboggling,
8) food blender, 9) twitchy,
10) mesmerising.

Page 8: Bye-bye Beeb!

Page 16: Richard Reviews...

1) ginormous, 2) wall poster, 3) theatre,
4) flamboyant, 5) revolutionary, 6) fearsome,
7) simplicity, 8) hypercar, 9) catapults, 10) dazzling.

Page 28: Italian Beauty

The correct order is 3, 7, 1, 4, 8, 6, 2, 5.

Page 29: Match the Outburst

Warwick Davis: 'Ooh, can't get it in gear.'
Rachel Riley: 'Come on, reasonably priced car!'
Joss Stone: 'Into fifth... give it some more welly...'
Al Murray: 'Turn, turn, turn, ya doughnut!'
Bill Bailey: 'Was that a crow? Or a raven?'
Johnny Vaughan: 'Don't lose your bottle! Keep your foot down!'
Amy Williams: 'OK, here we go. Skeleton run, but in a car.'

Page 30: James Reviews...

1) nerds, 2) aluminium, 3) impeccably,
4) yobbishness, 5) enthusiasts, 6) carbon fibre
7) peppered, 8) tremendous, 9) ludicrously,
10) excellence.

Page 35: Jiggled Jaguar

Page 40: Supersized Supercar Grid

Page 42: The Stig Drives

1) KTSSH! 2) SKRRREEE-whump! 3) KDUNK-KSSSSHHH 4) Clatter-dunk-tsh! 5) Squeeeeee!
6) SqueeeeAARGH-frunnk-fudunk-fudunk!
7) VNNNN! VRRRNG! 8) RRAAAARRRRGH!
9) NEEEyooowww 10) RRRRRRRUURRNN...

Page 48: Expensive Things with Bits Missing

Did you really need this answered? OK... plate, leg, saddle, shoes, about 10m of road, clock hands, windows, torch.

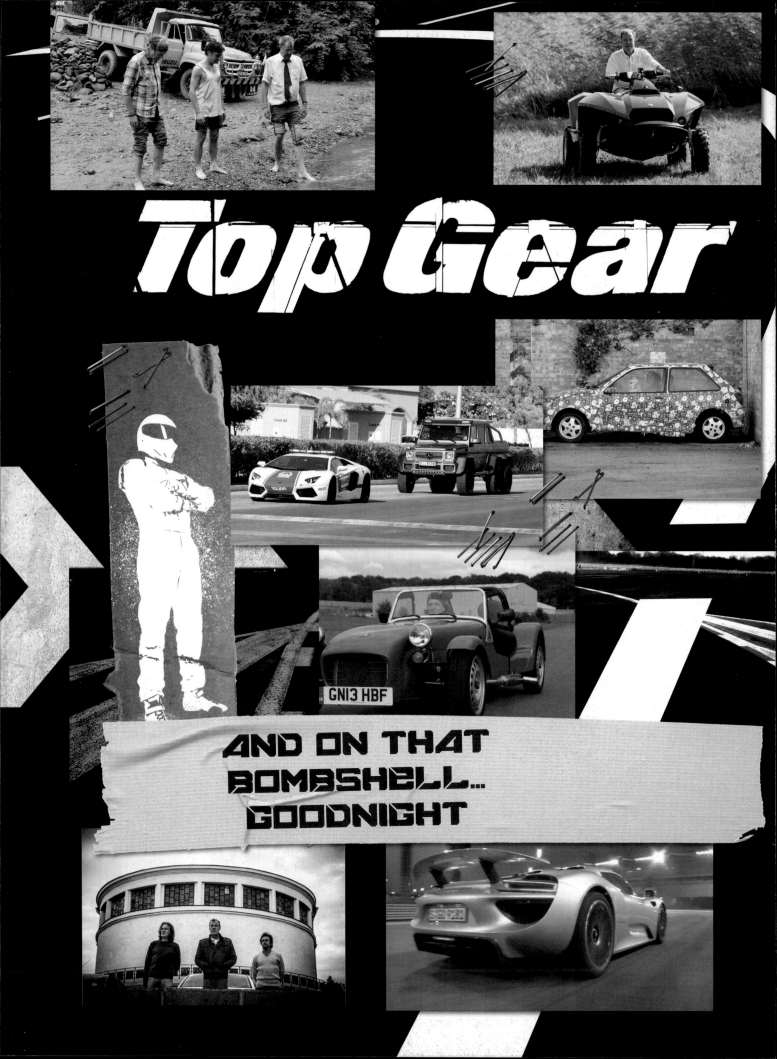

Top Gear

AND ON THAT BOMBSHELL... GOODNIGHT